Look out for these other exciting titles from Book House

The Danger Zone™

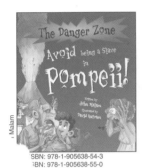

Malam

ISBN: 978-1-905638-54-3
ISBN: 978-1-905638-55-0

Fiona Macdonald

HB ISBN: 1-904642-75-6
PB ISBN: 1-904642-76-4

Jacqueline Morley

HB ISBN: 1-905087-55-1
PB ISBN: 1-905087-56-X

Fiona Macdonald

HB ISBN: 978-1-904642-11-4
PB ISBN: 978-1-904642-12-1

David Stewart

HB ISBN: 1-905087-57-8
PB ISBN: 1-905087-58-6

a Mary

HB ISBN: 978-1-905638-79-6
PB ISBN: 978-1-905638-80-2

Simon Smith

HB ISBN: 1-904194-81-8
PB ISBN: 1-904194-82-6

John Malam

HB ISBN: 1-904194-18-4
PB ISBN: 1-904194-19-2

David Stewart

HB ISBN: 1-904194-16-8
PB ISBN: 1-904194-17-6

Peter Cook

HB ISBN: 1-904642-13-6
PB ISBN: 1-904642-14-4

Jacqu

HB ISBN: 978-1-906370-25-1
PB ISBN: 978-1-906370-26-8

Ian Graham

HB ISBN: 1-904194-55-9
PB ISBN: 1-904194-56-7

Jacqueline Morley

HB ISBN: 1-904642-01-2
PB ISBN: 1-904642-02-0

Michael Ford

HB ISBN: 1-904642-05-5
PB ISBN: 1-904642-06-3

Fiona Macdonald

HB ISBN: 1-904194-53-2
PB ISBN: 1-904194-54-0

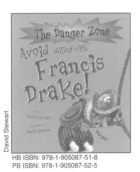

David Stewart

HB ISBN: 978-1-905087-51-8
PB ISBN: 978-1-905087-52-5

Jim Pipe

HB ISBN: 978-1-906714-66-6
PB ISBN: 978-1-906714-67-3

David Stewart

HB ISBN: 978-1-905638-04-8
PB ISBN: 978-1-905638-05-5

Fiona Macdonald

HB ISBN: 978-1-906370-99-2
PB ISBN: 978-1-906714-00-0

Mark Bergin

HB ISBN: 978-1-905087-61-7
PB ISBN: 978-1-905087-62-4

Fiona Macdonald

HB ISBN: 978-1-904642-07-7
PB ISBN: 978-1-904642-08-4

Fiona Macdonald

HB ISBN: 978-1-905087-49-5
PB ISBN: 978-1-905087-50-1

HB ISBN: 978-1-906714-17-8
PB ISBN: 978-1-906714-18-5

HB ISBN: 978-1-906714-09-3
PB ISBN: 978-1-906714-10-9

John Malam

HB ISBN: 978-1-904642-09-1
PB ISBN: 978-1-904642-10-7

domingo21
s - marzo 2004

SALSITAS
www.gruposalsitas.com
DE LA RAMBLA N 22 - 08001 - BARCELONA - Tel: 93 318 08 40 - GRUPOS Y RESERVAS : 902 888 115 - e-mail: info@gruposalsitas.com

Nou de la Rambla, 22 08001 BARCELONA
Tel. 93 318 08 40 • E-mail: info@gruposalsitas.com

`DJ RESIDENT
TONI BASS
RESTAURANTE CLUB
ABIERTO TODOS LOS DIAS DE 20:00Hs A 2:30Hs
VIERNES, SABADO Y VISPERAS FESTIVO HASTA LAS 3:00Hs
LUNES CERRAMOS

❶ Para pasarlo bien

 Fíjate en estos documentos. ¿Qué crees que anuncian?

UNA PELÍCULA   UN CONCIERTO   UN MERCADILLO
UN RESTAURANTE   UNA OBRA DE TEATRO
UN LOCAL DE COPAS   UN FESTIVAL
UN ESPECTÁCULO MUSICAL, DE DANZA, DE HUMOR ...

Ahora, escucha a estas personas. ¿Cuál de las actividades de estas páginas les gustaría hacer el fin de semana?

1. MARTA: _____
2. PABLO: _____
3. JUAN ENRIQUE: _____
4. LORETO: _____
5. CARMIÑA: _____

¿Y a ti? ¿Cuál de estos planes te interesa más?

• A mí me gustaría cenar en el restaurante Salsitas y después me quedaría ahí mismo para bailar y tomar una copa.

GANADORA DE 5 PREMIOS GOYA
Mejor Película • Mejor Director • Mejor Actor Javier Bardem
Mejor Actor de Reparto Luis Tosar • Mejor Actor Revelación José Ángel Egido

GANADORA DE LA CONCHA DE ORO
DEL FESTIVAL INTERNACIONAL DE CINE DE SAN SEBASTIÁN

Una producción Elías Querejeta y Jaume Roures-Mediapro

los lunes al sol

Javier Bardem Luis Tosar José Ángel Egido Nieve de Medina
Enrique Villén Celso Bugallo Joaquín Climent Aída Folch Serge Riaboukine
Guion Fernando León de Aranoa e Ignacio del Moral
Dirección Fernando León de Aranoa

**El retablo
de las maravillas**
Cinco variaciones sobre un tema de Cervantes

ELS JOGLARS

❷ Los sábados por la noche
¿Qué sueles hacer los sábados por la noche? ¿Alguna de estas cosas? Coméntalo con tus compañeros.

	normalmente	a veces	casi (nunca)
Voy a algún concierto.			
Voy al teatro.			
Voy al cine.			
Voy a tomar algo.			
Salgo a cenar.			
Me quedo en casa viendo la tele.			
Voy a casa de algún amigo.			
Voy a bailar.			
Otras cosas:			

• Yo salgo con mis amigos a tomar algo, o voy al cine.
○ Yo, normalmente, los sábados por la noche me quedo en casa y...

3 Los planes de Valentín

Es viernes y esta noche Valentín no sabe qué hacer. Tiene ganas de salir y ha escuchado a algunos de sus compañeros de trabajo que hacen planes.

VALENTÍN ES MUY AFICIONADO AL FÚTBOL Y NO LE GUSTA DEMASIADO IR AL CINE.

ESTÁ UN POCO GORDO, TIENE COLESTEROL Y ESTÁ A DIETA.

ACABA DE ROMPER CON ELENA, SU NOVIA, Y ESTÁ UN POCO TRISTE.

NO SOPORTA BAILAR PERO, EN CAMBIO, LE ENCANTA LA MÚSICA.

NORMALMENTE, LOS SÁBADOS SALE CON ALGUIEN A TOMAR ALGO.

LE GUSTA CLARA.

1

¿Por qué no te vienes?

No puedo, es que ya he quedado...

Clara — Tina

2

¿Qué hacéis esta noche?

Pablo quiere ver el partido...

Claudia — Lola

3

¿Adónde vamos? ¿Qué te apetece hacer?

Alejandro — Federico

4

Quería reservar una mesa para esta noche...

Beatriz — Ramón

■ GUÍA DEL OCIO ■

■ ÁNGELES CAÍDOS

General Ramos, 3.
Cócteles, humor
y karaoke hasta
las 3h de la
madrugada.
Tarjetas.
Lunes cerrado.

■ EL SÉPTIMO CIELO

**Cenas con música clásica.
Venus, 15 (esquina Peligro) tel. 902 345 611.
Párking clientes.
Especialidad en buey a la parrilla y marisco.
Menú gastronómico: 42 euros. Abierto de 8h a 1.30h. Viernes y sábados hasta 2.30h.**

■ RESTAURANTE PIZZERÍA MASTROPIERO

Cocina italoargentina. Ensaladas, pizzas y carnes. Tel. 902 22 46 78.

HABANA CLUB

Tapas y copas

Salsa y jazz en vivo

Precios jóvenes
en un ambiente tropical
Mahón, 21
(metro: Bilbao / bus 45 y 32)

RETRANSMISIÓN DESDE EL ESTADIO SANTIAGO BERNABÉU

HOY a las **22.00h** en **Antena 5**

REAL MADRID - F.C. BARCELONA

Actividades

A Escucha las cuatro conversaciones de los compañeros de trabajo de Valentín. ¿Qué van a hacer?

Clara   No lo sabe.
Tina _____
Claudia y Lola _____
Federico y Alejandro _____
Ramón y Beatriz _____

B Fíjate en la información que tienes sobre Valentín. ¿Con quién crees que puede salir esta noche?

	sí	no	¿por qué?
con Clara			
con Tina			
con Claudia y con Lola			
con Federico y con Alejandro			
con Ramón y con Beatriz			

C ¿Te has fijado en cómo se hacen las siguientes cosas en estas cuatro conversaciones? Vuélvelas a escuchar y trata de anotarlo.

1. Expresar el deseo de hacer algo.
2. Proponer una cita.
3. Proponer una actividad.
4. Rechazar una invitación.

gente que lo pasa bien

4 Cine

¿Cuál es la última película que has ido a ver? ¿Has visto alguna de la siguiente lista? Añade tus tres películas favoritas. A continuación, piensa en una de ellas y di alguna cosa sin mencionar el título. Tus compañeros tienen que adivinarla.

• Es una película de ciencia ficción y sale Keanu Reeves. Es buenísima.
○ ¡Matrix!
• Sí.

El Deseo presenta, con la colaboración de TVE y Canal+

un film de ALMODÓVAR

La Mala Educación

GAEL GARCÍA BERNAL   FELE MARTÍNEZ   DANIEL GIMÉNEZ CACHO
LLUIS HOMAR   FRANCISCO BOIRA   JAVIER CÁMARA
José Luis Alcaine   José Salcedo   Alberto Iglesias
Esther García   Agustín Almodóvar
Escrita y Dirigida por PEDRO ALMODÓVAR
www.lamalaeducacion.com

LA MALA EDUCACION
ROLL   SCENE   TAKE

El señor de los anillos
Casablanca
Harry Potter
Titanic
La mala educación
El Padrino

_____

_____

_____

Imagina que esta noche puedes ver una de ellas. ¿Cuál elegirías? ¿Por qué? ¿Cuál es la película que más interesa a nuestra clase? ¿Votamos?

• A mí, la que me gustaría volver a ver es El señor de los anillos. Me encantan las películas de aventuras.

5 ¿Habéis visto *Hable con ella*?

Si te gusta el cine, seguro que puedes recomendar alguna película a tus compañeros. Descríbela y da tu opinión.

• ¿Habéis visto *Hable con ella*? Es una película de Almodóvar. Es un drama... Los actores son muy buenos... Está muy bien... A mí me encantó.
○ Yo no la he visto.
■ Yo sí. A mí también me gustó mucho.

También puedes recomendar a tus compañeros un lugar o una actividad de la ciudad donde te encuentras.

**UN BAR MUSICAL   UNA OBRA DE TEATRO   UNA TIENDA NUEVA
UN RESTAURANTE   UNA CAFETERÍA   UNA PELÍCULA DE LA CARTELERA
UNA CALLE PARA PASEAR   UNA DISCOTECA   UN CONCIERTO**

• Pues el otro día descubrí un restaurante de cocina vasca muy bueno...
○ ¿Ah sí? ¿Dónde?
• Al lado de la Catedral. ¡Pedí una merluza que estaba...!

**VALORAR Y DESCRIBIR
UN ESPECTÁCULO**

- - - - - - - - - - - - - - - - - -

● ¿Habéis visto *Matrix Revolution?*
○ Yo no la he visto.
  Yo sí, es...
  genial / buenísima / divertidísima/...
  bastante buena / interesante/...
  un rollo.
  muy mala.

A mí   me encantó.
       me gustó bastante.
       no me gustó nada.

Es un tipo de cine   que no soporto.
             teatro
             concierto
             música

No soporto ese tipo de   películas.
                 teatro.

Es una comedia.
    un *thriller*.
    una película de acción.
              del oeste.
              de aventuras.
              de guerra.
              de terror.
              de ciencia ficción.
              policíaca.

El **director es** Julio Medem.
= **Es una película de** Julio Medem.

El **protagonista es** Antonio Banderas.

Sale Victoria Abril.

Trata de un periodista que va a Bosnia y... = **Va de** un periodista que va a Bosnia y...

**PONERSE DE ACUERDO
PARA HACER ALGO**

- - - - - - - - - - - - - - - - - -

Preguntar a los demás.
¿*Adónde podemos ir?*
¿*Qué te/le/os/les apetece hacer?*
¿*Adónde te/le/os/les gustaría ir?*

Proponer.
¿*Por qué no* vamos al cine?
¿*Y si* vamos a cenar por ahí?
¿*Te/os/le/les apetece* ir a tomar algo?

Aceptar.
Vale.
Buena idea. Me apetece.

Excusarse.

Es que hoy **no puedo.**
esta noche **no me va bien.**

Hoy no puedo.
Pero podemos quedar
para otro día.

Es que esta
tarde me va fatal. ¿Nos
llamamos y quedamos
otro día?

Pues no sé si voy a
poder... Si veo que puedo,
te llamo, ¿vale?

DESEOS DE HACER ALGO

Me gustaría dormir todo el día.
ir a nadar.
Me apetece ir a un concierto de jazz.
ver esa película.

Podemos ir
a bailar. A ti te
encanta bailar...

Sí, pero
hoy no me
apetece
nada.

Apetecer funciona como **gustar.**
Me **apetece** ir al cine.
Me **apetecen** unas aceitunas.

**Consultorio gramatical,
páginas 133 a 136.**

6 La caja tonta

Esta es la programación de una cadena de
televisión española durante un día. ¿Puedes
deducir qué tipo de programa es cada uno?
¿Esta programación se parece a la de tu país?

6.30	Informativos Telecinco
9.25	Desayunamos con...
11.00	Mesa de debate
14.30	Informativos Telecinco
15.30	Corazón, corazón
16.30	Gran hermano
17.30	Sesión de tarde: *Troya*
19.45	50 x 15
20.30	Informativos Telecinco
21.30	Siete vidas (Capítulo 4)
22.30	At. Madrid - Barça
00.30	La noche de Fuentes
2.00	Informativos Telecinco
2.30	Teletienda
5.30	Planeta vivo

¿Y a ti, cuáles son los programas que más
te gustan? ¿Cuáles no soportas?

• A mí me gusta mucho Gran Hermano. También se hace en mi país.
¡Y no soporto los debates en televisión!
○ Pues yo no soporto los programas como Gran Hermano. Y me
encantan los del corazón. El que más me gusta de mi país se
llama *Reality heart.*

7 Me encantaría pero...

En la vida, muchas veces hay que dar excusas. Para practicar cómo
excusarnos cuando nos invitan, jugaremos un poco. Escribe en cuatro
papelitos dos propuestas o dos invitaciones y dos excusas para esas
propuestas. El profesor las mezclará y las volverá a repartir. Cada uno
lee una propuesta, y los que tengan la excusa adecuada, reaccionan.

• ¿Te apetece ir al cine esta tarde? A mí me gustaría ver *Titanic.*

○ Esta tarde no me va bien. Tengo que ir al médico...

8 Un domingo ideal

Escucha a estos españoles que describen su domingo ideal.
¿De cuáles de estos momentos hablan?

	1	2	3
hora de levantarse	X		
desayuno			
durante la mañana			
comida			
después de comer			
durante la tarde			
cena			
por la noche			

Imagina ahora que el próximo domingo puedes hacer todo lo que
más te gusta, esas cosas que normalmente no sueles hacer. ¿Qué
harías? Piénsalo un poco y, luego, explícaselo a tus compañeros.

• Yo me levantaría tarde, a las once, y desayunaría en la cama...

9 Un fin de semana en Madrid

Vamos a imaginar que toda la clase pasa un fin de semana en Madrid. Hay que planear las actividades. Leed todas estas informaciones que aparecen en la revista *Gente de Madrid*.

MADRID DÍA Y NOCHE ||||||

Madrid es una de las ciudades con más vida de Europa. El clima y el carácter de los madrileños han hecho proliferar muchos locales dedicados al ocio. Además de las posibilidades de diversión concretas -zoo, parques de atracciones, museos, etc.- hay innumerables bares, discotecas, *cabarets, after hours* y locales de música en vivo. En especial si visita la capital de España en primavera o en verano, prepárese para acostarse muy tarde, pues poquísimas ciudades en el mundo tienen una vida nocturna como la de Madrid. En Madrid se sale a cenar entre las 10 y las 11. Se acude a un bar hasta más o menos las 2 y luego se va a una o varias discotecas. Algunas cierran a altas horas de la madrugada.

VISITAS DE INTERÉS

EL MADRID DE LOS AUSTRIAS
Los edificios más antiguos de Madrid (s. XVI). Pequeñas plazas y las calles con más encanto de la ciudad, ideales para recorrer a pie.

LA GRAN VÍA
El centro de Madrid por excelencia, una calle que nunca duerme. Cafeterías, cines, tiendas, librerías...

LA PLAZA DE SANTA ANA
Centro favorito de reunión de los turistas y estudiantes extranjeros. Ofrece una enorme variedad de bares de tapas, restaurantes, cafés, clubs de jazz, pensiones y hoteles.

EL BARRIO DE SALAMANCA
Una de las zonas más elegantes de Madrid. Tiendas lujosas en calles como Serrano o Velázquez, restaurantes...

EL PALACIO REAL (s. XVIII)
En su interior se pueden admirar cuadros de Goya y de artistas franceses, italianos y españoles. C/ Bailén. De lunes a sábado: 9-18h. Festivos: 9-15h.

LA PUERTA DEL SOL
El centro oficial del territorio español, donde se halla el Km 0 de la red viaria. Bares, tiendas y mucha animación.

EL BARRIO DE CHUECA
El distrito que nunca duerme. La modernidad de Madrid se concentra en sus calles. Restaurantes de diseño, las mejores tiendas de la ciudad, clubs de noche, terrazas...

EL BARRIO DE MALASAÑA
Ambiente bohemio y *underground* en bares de rock y en cafés literarios abiertos hasta la madrugada.

EL PASEO DE RECOLETOS Y LA CASTELLANA
Los edificios más modernos de Madrid, como las sedes de los grandes bancos, la Torre Picasso o las Torres KIO.

EL PARQUE DE EL RETIRO
Un parque enorme con agradables paseos y un lago para remar.

EN CARTEL

SARA BARAS EN MARIANA PINEDA
Sobre una idea de Federico García Lorca y con coreografía de Sara Baras vuelve a Madrid *Mariana Pineda*. 6 únicas funciones. Teatro Lope de Vega (Gran Vía, 57). De martes a jueves, 21h; de viernes a domingo, 22h. Precio: 36 euros.

ARTE Y CULTURA

GABRIEL GARCÍA MÁRQUEZ
Conferencia del escritor G. García Márquez en el Círculo de Bellas Artes: "El concepto de realidad en la narrativa hispanoamericana". Domingo, 18h.

CENTRO DE ARTE REINA SOFÍA
Santa Isabel, 52. Tel. 914 675 062. http://museoreinasofia.mcu.es Organiza interesantes exposiciones de arte contemporáneo que incluyen las últimas vanguardias. Cierra los martes.

MUSEO DEL PRADO
Paseo del Prado. Tel. 913 302 800. http://museoprado.mcu.es. Horario: de martes a domingo, de 9 a 19h. Lunes cerrado. La mejor pinacoteca del mundo. Posee las incomparables colecciones de Goya, Velázquez, El Greco...

TYSSEN-BORNEMISZA
Paseo del Prado, 8. Tel. 913 690 151. www.museothyssen.org. De martes a domingo de 10 a 19h. La mejor colección privada de pintura europea.

DE NOCHE

MOBY DICK CLUB
www.mobydickclub.com. Sala de conciertos, con una original decoración, donde se realizan actuaciones de música en directo. Los lunes a partir de las 23.30h, sesiones a la carta: el público escoge los temas que quiere que toque la banda de música.

LOLITA
www.lolitalounge.net. Ritmos electrónicos, disco y *funk* en dos plantas. Ambientado en la estética de la Dolce Vita y decorado a lo retro, este local ofrece planes alternativos para el ocio: los viernes, proyección de cortometrajes; los jueves, café-teatro y una vez al mes, pasarela de las últimas creaciones de jóvenes diseñadores de moda.

CHOCOLATE
C. Barbieri, 15. Tel. 915 220 133. www.interocio.es/chocolate. Este café-restaurante, situado en Chueca, ofrece una cocina imaginativa, además de un cocktail-bar. Menú de día y de noche.

TABERNA CASA PATAS
C. Cañizares, 10. Tel. 913 690 496. www.casapatas.com. Las noches de flamenco con más duende de Madrid, con artistas de la talla de Remedios Amaya o Niña Pastori, en un tablao nunca saturado por autobuses de turistas. Antes y durante el espectáculo se sirven tapas de jamón, queso, lomo o chorizo, platos de pescadito frito, entrecots y la especialidad de la casa: rabo de toro. Horario de restaurante de lunes a domingo: de 12 a 17h y de 20 a 2h. Espectáculo: L, M, X y J a las 22.30h. V y S a las 24h.

MONTANA
C. Lagasca, 5. Tel. 914 359 901. Restaurante de cocina mediterránea, donde puede degustar los productos de la temporada, la magia de una cocina directa y natural: huevos estrellados, aves y bacalao son algunas de sus especialidades. Menú a mediodía.

DEPORTES

LIGA DE CAMPEONES
Final de la *Champions League* en Madrid. Sábado a las 21h. Estadio Santiago Bernabéu. Entradas: 912 222 345.

CASA PATAS

El punto de referencia del mundo
del flamenco en Madrid

Restaurante con espectáculo en vivo

C/. Canizares, 10 - 28012 Madrid
Teléfono: 91 369 04 96 / 91 369 33 94
Fax: 91 360 02 00
E- mail: cpatas@conservatorioflamenco.org

LA FUSIÓN

laboratorio de sensaciones,
rico en temperaturas, sabores
y texturas

www.lafusionmadrid.com
Reservas. 91 571 91 72

chocolate
restaurante

d e   l u n e s   a   j u e v e s :
menú mediodía 8,90 €
menú noche 16,00 €

barbieri 15 . tfn: 915 220 133
chueca 28004 madrid
www.interocio.es/chocolate

II FESTIVAL DE CORTOMETRAJES

Lolit 35 m

MAYO DÍAS: 5, 12, 19 Y 26
PROYECCIÓN DE LOS CORTOMETRAJES,
DE LOS CUALES 12 PASARÁN A LA FINAL.
VOTACIÓN DEL PÚBLICO ASISTENTE

JUNIO DÍAS: 2, 9, 16, 23 Y 30
PROYECCIÓN DE LOS CORTOMETRAJES FINALISTAS
DÍA 30 NOCHE DE CLAUSURA Y ENTREGA DE PREMIOS

Escribe tus preferencias para el fin de semana.

viernes por la noche   sábado por la mañana   comida del sábado
sábado por la tarde   sábado por la noche   domingo por la mañana
comida del domingo   domingo por la tarde

Puedes obtener más información escuchando el programa de radio
"Gente divertida", o buscando información en Internet; así podrás
completar o modificar tus planes para el fin de semana.

Dónde y cuándo.
El *concierto* **es** a las 8h.
El *concierto* **es** en el Teatro
Real.

Para concertar una cita.
¿Cómo
¿A qué hora } **quedamos?**
¿Dónde

¿Quedamos en mi hotel?
¿Te/os/le/les va bien...
    ... delante del cine?
    ... a las seis?
    ... el sábado?

**Para proponer otro lugar
u otro momento.**
(Me iría) mejor...
Preferiría...
    ... un poco más tarde.
    ... la tarde.
    ... en el centro.

Para hablar de una cita.
He quedado a las 3h **con**
María **en** su hotel **para** ir
al Prado.

10 ¿Qué queréis hacer?
Cada uno explica las cosas que más le apetece hacer y busca compañeros
para hacerlas. Luego, tendréis que organizar las citas: decidir la hora, el
lugar, quién reserva o saca las entradas, etc.

● Pues a mí, el sábado por la mañana me gustaría ir de compras
   al barrio de Chueca. ¿A alguien más le apetece?
○ A mí.
● Pues podemos ir juntos, si quieres.
○ Vale, ¿a qué hora quedamos? ¿A las 10h?
● Mejor un poco más tarde. ¿Qué tal a las 11h?
○ Perfecto.

Para acordarte de todo, puedes resumir los datos de las citas del modo siguiente.

He quedado con _____
para _____
Hemos quedado en _____ a las _____
Tengo que_____

11 El próximo sábado

¿Y en el lugar donde estamos estudiando español? ¿Qué se puede hacer el
próximo fin de semana? Comentadlo y anotad las propuestas más interesantes.
También podéis buscar información (en Internet o en la prensa) sobre la
oferta de ocio de alguna ciudad donde se habla español.

gente que lo pasa bien

Fin de semana en la calle

A los extranjeros que visitan España les llama mucho la atención la cantidad de gente que ha+y en la calle. Y la cantidad de bares.

Es seguramente la versión urbana moderna de la tradición mediterránea del ágora, de la plaza como lugar de encuentro. Y es que el "*hobby* nacional" es, sin duda alguna, hablar. Se habla en la calle, en los restaurantes, en las terrazas, con los amigos o con la familia. Y se habla generalmente en torno a una mesa, o en una barra de bar, casi siempre bebiendo o comiendo.

Los fines de semana mucha gente huye de las grandes ciudades. Son muchos los que tienen una segunda residencia, en el campo o en la playa. Muchas familias se reúnen en la antigua casa familiar, en el pueblo. El problema es la vuelta a casa el domingo. Sufrir un atasco impresionante para entrar en la ciudad es casi inevitable.

Los que se quedan en la ciudad salen. Y salen mucho. Por ejemplo, al mediodía, antes de comer, van a tomar el aperitivo. Un paseo, unas cañas y unas tapas en una terraza, al sol, son para muchos el máximo placer de un domingo. Luego, se come en familia, muy tarde, sobre las tres o pasadas las tres. Se come en la propia casa, en la de los abuelos, o en casa de los tíos o de los hermanos. O si no, en un restaurante.

Por las tardes hay larguísimas colas en los cines y las calles céntricas están llenas de paseantes.

Las noches de los viernes y de los sábados las ciudades están también muy animadas y hay tráfico hasta la madrugada: gente que va o que viene de los restaurantes, gente que entra o sale de los espectáculos y grupos de jóvenes que van a bailar o a tomar algo.

Otra de las cosas que puede sorprender al visitante es lo poco planificado que está el ocio. Muchas veces nos encontramos con alguien, sin haber decidido muy bien qué vamos a hacer. Nos citamos a una hora no muy exacta ("a eso de las nueve", "sobre las diez"...) y luego "ya veremos". Se toma algo en un sitio y, al cabo de un rato, el grupo se traslada a otro lugar, lo que también sorprende a muchos extranjeros. Y es que, para los españoles, es más importante con quién se está que dónde se está.

En los últimos años la práctica de deportes se ha puesto de moda y son muchos también los que organizan su tiempo libre y sus fines de semana en torno a su deporte favorito: la bicicleta o el tenis, el esquí o el golf, el *jogging*, el fútbol o la vela... Pero, ojo, siempre con amigos... Y hablando.

12 Observa las fotos y coméntalas con tus compañeros. ¿Hay cosas que os sorprenden?

13 Lee el texto. ¿Puedes relacionar las imágenes con algunas de las informaciones que da?

14 ¿Qué es igual y qué es diferente en tu cultura?

Author:

Jacqueline Morley studied English at Oxford University. She has taught English and History, and now works as a freelance writer. She has written historical fiction and non-fiction for children.

Illustrator:

John James was born in London in 1959. He studied at Eastbourne College of Art and has specialised in historical reconstruction since leaving art school in 1982.

Series creator:

David Salariya is an illustrator, designer and author. He is the founder of the Salariya Book Company, which specialises in the creation and publication of books for young people, from babies to teenagers, under its imprints Book House, Scribblers and Scribo.

Consultant:

Dr. Simon James is Reader in Archaeology at the University of Leicester. He has excavated widely on prehistoric, Roman and medieval sites, including Roman villas in Italy and Britain. He is a specialist in the history and archaeology of the Roman Empire, in particular of the Roman army and of the north-western provinces.

Editor: **Vicki Power**

© The Salariya Book Company Ltd MMX
All rights reserved. No part of this publication may be reproduced, stored in or introduced into a retrieval system or transmitted in any form, or by any means (electronic, mechanical, photocopying, recording or otherwise) without the written permission of the publisher. Any person who does any unauthorised act in relation to this publication may be liable to criminal prosecution and civil claims for damages.

Published by
Book House, an imprint of
The Salariya Book Company Ltd
25 Marlborough Place, Brighton BN1 1UB

$ALARIYA

Visit our website at **www.book-house.co.uk**
or go to **www.salariya.com**
for **free** electronic versions of:
You Wouldn't Want to be an Egyptian Mummy!
You Wouldn't Want to be a Roman Gladiator!
You Wouldn't Want to be a Polar Explorer!
You Wouldn't Want to sail on a 19th-Century Whaling Ship!

ISBN 978-1-906714-58-1

A CIP catalogue record for this book is available from the British Library.

Printed and bound in China.

CONTENTS

PAPER FROM
SUSTAINABLE
FORESTS

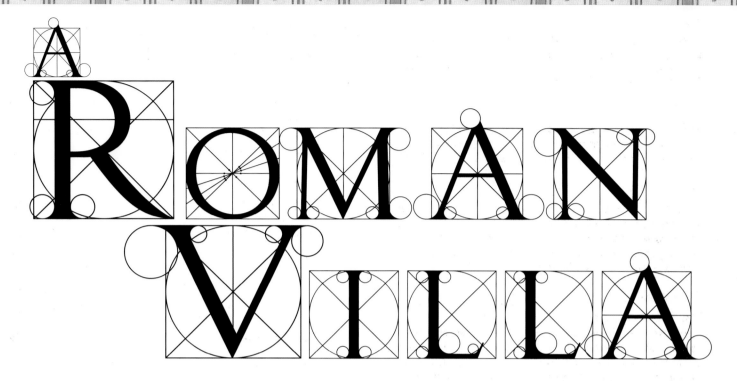

A ROMAN VILLA

Written by
Jacqueline Morley

Series created by
David Salariya

Illustrated by
John James

BOOK HOUSE

INTRODUCTION

WHAT IS A VILLA? Today the word may make us think of a holiday home, perhaps by the sea. If you had lived in nineteenth-century England you would have taken it to mean quite a grand detached house, of the kind that was being built on the outskirts of towns or in the neighbouring countryside, for successful businessmen to live in. These people were being slightly snobbish calling their houses 'villas', because the word had been in use for many centuries to describe a country house on an estate belonging to a rich and usually aristocratic landowner. The same word had been used with very nearly the same meaning in Roman times.

To the Romans a villa was not just a building. It was also the farm estate that surrounded it. The earliest Roman villas were small farms, and many later ones were too. Ancient Roman history spans so many centuries, and its empire covered such a vast area, that it is not possible to choose one villa typical of so many times and climates. This book tells you about life on a wealthy Roman's villa, in the Italian countryside, at a time when the Roman empire was peaceful and prosperous, in the first century AD.

VILLA HISTORY

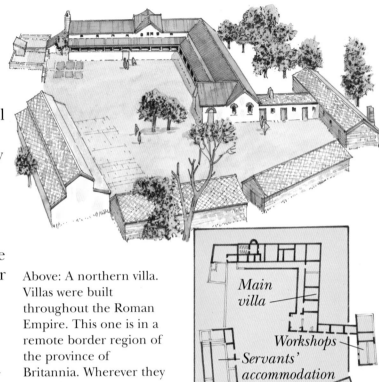

IN ROME'S EARLY CENTURIES many Romans owned just enough land to grow food for their families and a little over to sell. The long wars with Rome's great rival Carthage, in the 3rd and 2nd centuries BC, ruined many of these small farmers. They could not farm while they were away fighting, and when they returned they had to compete with town-dwelling profiteers who had been buying land to create big farming villas.

These new-style owners used slaves to do the farm work. There were plenty of slaves in later Republican times (3rd to 1st centuries BC), for prisoners of war were being sold as slaves. Many Romans grew used to thinking of work as something done only by slaves and uneducated people. The best way to live, they believed, was to own slaves whose work made a profit, enabling their owners to spend time in government and politics, and in reading, talking and enjoying themselves.

Above: A northern villa. Villas were built throughout the Roman Empire. This one is in a remote border region of the province of Britannia. Wherever they went, the Romans encouraged people to copy Roman ways.

Above: Plan of the northern villa. Its remains were found at Llantwit Major in Glamorgan, Wales. They date from the 3rd and 4th centuries AD.

Left: A commercial farm. This villa near Pompeii, of the 1st century BC, contained rooms for slaves but no luxury accommodation.

Left: A seaside villa, based on Roman wall paintings. From the 1st century BC the coastline south of Rome was lined with elegant holiday houses.

Above: An African villa, from an early 4th-century mosaic from Tabarka, Tunisia. The building has lookout towers and is set in an orchard. There are ducks by a stream.

City landowners had to visit their villas from time to time, to make sure that their slave overseers were running things well and not cheating them. From the 1st century BC onwards it grew fashionable for owners and their families to spend part of the summer at their villas. Very rich Romans spent vast sums of money on villas that were holiday houses and had no farms.

Odeon (theatre)

The villa at Tivoli, near Rome, designed by the Emperor Hadrian in the 2nd century BC as a holiday palace in which he hoped to escape the cares of government.

Palace

Stadium

Baths

Canopus pool

Hadrian's villa had gardens, theatres, army barracks, libraries, sports grounds and even underground roads. Some of it is still standing.

Pool

Pool with island

Dining room

Greek and Latin libraries

Nymphaeum

BRITANNIA

GERMANIA

GALLIA

CAPPADOCIA

HISPANIA

Rome

MAURETANIA

ITALIA

MACEDONIA

ASIA

AFRICA PROCONSULARIS

AEGYPTUS

264 BC *At start of wars with Carthage*

AD 14 *Added by end of rule of Augustus*

133 BC *After the wars, and the taking of Spain*

AD 180 *Added by end of rule of Marcus Aurelius*

Above: This map shows how the Roman Empire grew during Republican and Imperial times.

Greek theatre

THE NEW VILLA

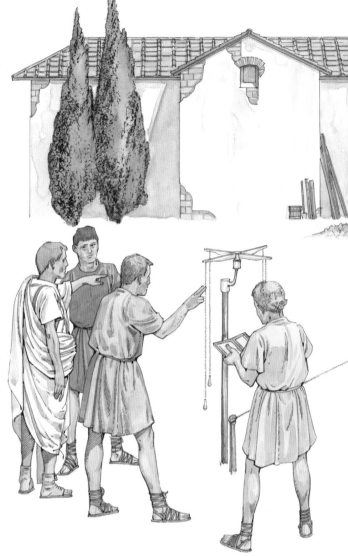

A RICH ROMAN has just bought a villa in the countryside south of Rome. The soil is good, there is a stream to supply water, and a town conveniently near for selling produce. Profits should be high. The owner means to come here often with his family, to enjoy the country air and fine views.

The previous owner had been very old-fashioned. He had lived in the simple style of bygone Republican times. His house had been small and plainly decorated, with no grand reception rooms and only one dining room. Worst of all, the rooms for baths were cramped and dark. It was not up to the standard that well-to-do people expected, so the new owner has had much of it pulled down to make way for a grander building. He has brought an architect from Rome to make plans, and is employing the best craftsmen to decorate the inside. The walls of the rooms will be painted with landscapes and lively scenes, and there will be mosaic on the floors. He has ordered expensive statues for the house and for the ornamental garden that is being laid out alongside the old orchard.

The slave quarters will be extended too, but these will have no special decorations.

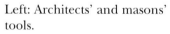

Left: Architects' and masons' tools.
1. Bronze dividers used in drawing plans.
2. Try-square.
3. Bronze folding ruler
4. Plumbline.
5. Dividers used in laying mosaic.

Right: Underfloor heating was installed in some rooms, including the baths (see pages 16–17). Hot air from furnaces flowed through a space under the floor, which was held up on brick columns.

1

3

2

4

5

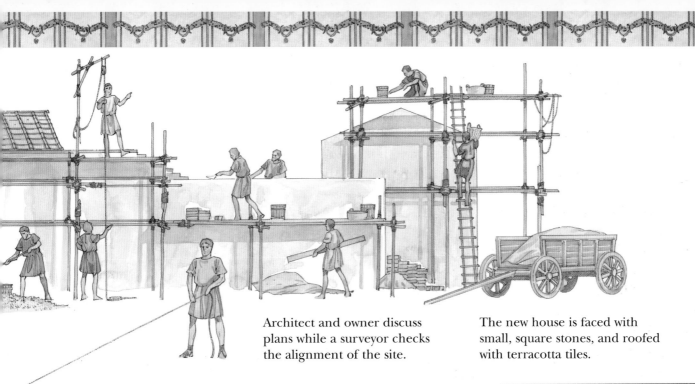

Architect and owner discuss plans while a surveyor checks the alignment of the site.

The new house is faced with small, square stones, and roofed with terracotta tiles.

Right: The *atrium*, or central hall, in early Roman houses had an inward-sloping roof with an opening to collect rainwater. Water supply was better by Imperial times, but atrium roofs were still built in this way.
1. Top view of atrium roof.
2. Roof cross-section.
3. Rainwater spouts.
4. Section showing spout.
5. Tiles.

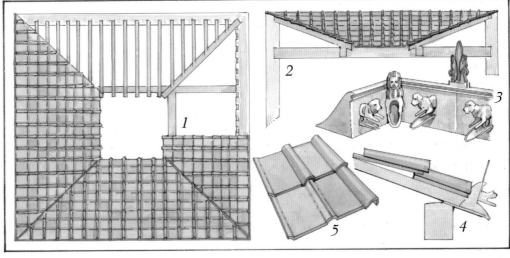

Left: Mosaic, which was used to decorate floors and walls, was made of tiny cubes of coloured stones and glass set in a layer of wet mortar.

Right: Walls were built of rubble bonded with clay, and limestone (1), and later of rubble and cement (2). Outside walls were faced with limestone (3) or small square stones (4). For corners, layers of brick and stone (5) were used. Partitions were timber-framed rubble (6).

THE HOUSE

The villa's layout shown here is based on Roman remains found at Montmaurin in south-west France, which are later than our imaginary owner's time, but show how a large villa was organised.

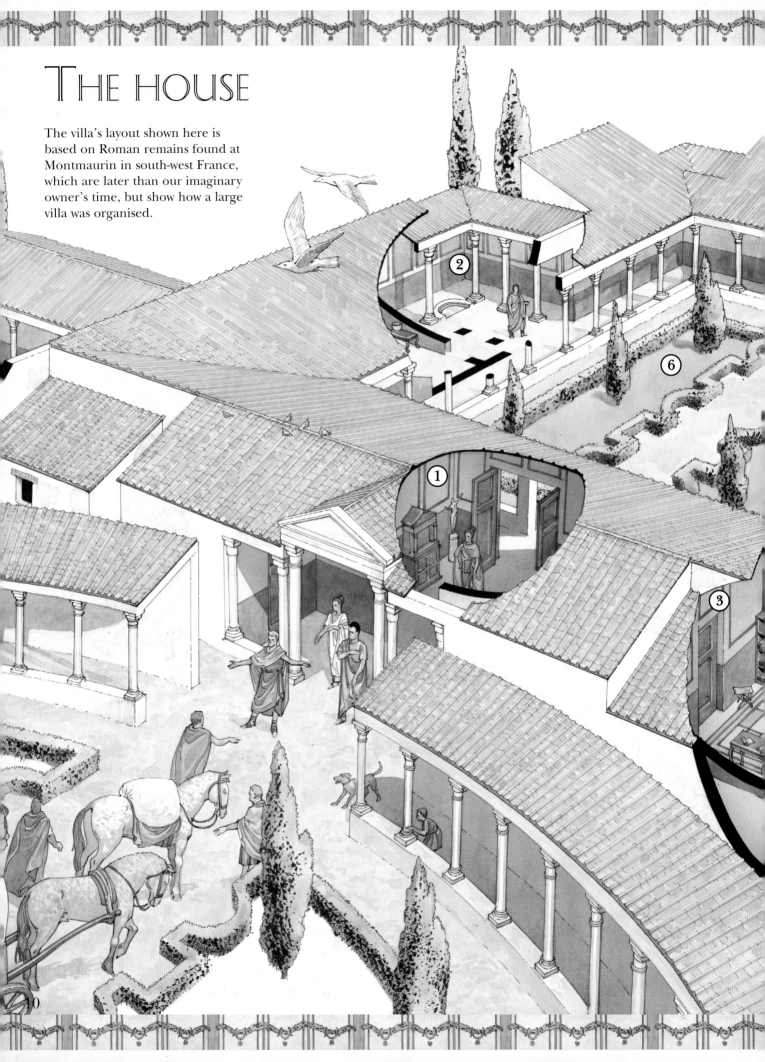

5. The winter dining room, which faced south to catch the sun. It also had underfloor heating. In the same position on the other side of the court was a cool, north-facing summer dining room.
6. The main courtyard, filled with ornamental hedges and trees.
7. An inner court, on either side of which lay a curved portico enclosing a little garden.
8. An open dining room, roofed with a trellis of vines.

THE VILLA is finished. Its new house is large and fine. This part of a villa was used only by the owner and his family. The part that held the slaves' quarters and the farm buildings was known as the *villa rustica* (country villa). Sometimes the two were combined in one building, but in elegant villas the villa rustica was tucked out of the way.

Visitors to the new house reached the pillared entrance porch by crossing a large courtyard surrounded by a shady colonnade. The owner might come to the entrance to greet important guests. Ordinary callers were asked their business by the doorkeeper, whose room was at the side of the porch. Official visitors were led into a reception hall inside the great double entrance doors. This room also opened into the first of the inner courtyards around which the house was built. On the left of this garden court lay a suite of richly decorated rooms for entertaining visitors. On the right were bedrooms for family and friends, and the owner's office and library. A passage to the left of the entrance led to a cool, refreshing courtyard, called a *nymphaeum*, with statues and splashing fountains. Beyond this were the baths and the villa rustica.

1. The reception hall, through which important visitors entered the house. The doors were normally kept shut. The domestic slaves came and went through a passage alongside this room.
2. A reception room in the form of an atrium. Its slightly sloping floor drained the rain from the roof into a small pool.
3. The library. Books were written on long rolls of papyrus. These were kept rolled up, on shelves or in cupboards. 4. A bedroom with a mosaic floor.

The people

THE OWNER has brought his family to see the new villa. They have just arrived from Rome and intend to stay some time. They have brought with them a few special slaves who are essential to the comforts of the family. The owner must have his personal manservant and his secretary. The secretary is very well educated, and more like a friend than a servant. The owner's wife and elder daughter will each need her own maidservant to attend her when she bathes, to dress her and look after her hair. The younger children's tutor must be there to give lessons. And of course the chef must come too, for there is no-one in the country who can cook the special dishes for which he is famous.

Above: The family's driver and horse-drawn carriage. Horses were expensive to keep. Poorer people used mules and donkeys.

Right: The tutor, the chef and the secretary.

Right and below: The owner and his family. Behind them, the family's household slaves. The three personal attendants stand just behind their owners. The owner's children have brought their pet dog with them. The younger daughter has brought her pet magpie as well.

All the household slaves were born as slaves of the family, except the chef, who was bought recently for a great deal of money. The slaves' parents had been slaves of the owner's father, who paid for the education of the one who is now secretary, since he was such a clever child.

Right: The goatherd, the swineherd and two of the field hands. The field hands do different jobs according to the time of year, usually working in small gangs. Each gang has a foreman who makes sure that nobody is slacking.

Left and below: The smith, the head gardener and the farm cook. The cook and her helpers cook for the farm workers. In front of them comes the chief vine dresser. He trains the grapevines, a highly skilled job. Standing alone is the head shepherd. In front of him are the overseer and his wife.

Above: The foremen of the olive pressroom and of the vine pressroom.

Right: The baker, who also grinds the flour.

The slaves who work at the villa have come to greet their new masters. They live here all the time and are part of the villa's farm equipment, just like the animals and the ploughs. Their value was taken into account in fixing the price that the new owner paid for the villa.

The overseer is the most important person on the farm. He is responsible for spending the money that the owner allows for the upkeep of the villa. He has to organise the work of the other slaves and make sure that there is a profit at the end of each year. His wife is in charge of the female slaves.

INSIDE THE HOUSE

LARGE ROMAN HOUSES of Imperial times (27 BC to AD 476) had many rooms, often arranged around one or more courtyards. A portico (covered walk supported by pillars) surrounded the courtyard and served as a passage by which you could reach all the rooms. The Romans copied this arrangement from the Greeks.

Wealthy Roman homes were highly decorated, but most of this ornament was provided by elaborately painted walls and mosaic floors. The Romans did not use nearly as much furniture as we do, though some rich people spent huge sums on such things as tables made of bronze, or of ivory and rare woods inlaid with tortoiseshell or gold. One Roman is reported to have spent half a million sesterces on a table – an enormous amount of money. The most important item of furniture was the couch or bed, on which people slept at night and reclined during the day to eat, read, write or receive visitors. Small side tables, benches and folding seats were moved about where necessary.

It was important in summer to keep out glaring light and heat. There were no fireplaces of the kind we are used to. Charcoal-burning braziers were brought into the room when it was chilly.

Right: Part of the owner's house, with areas of the roof cut away to show the rooms and furniture.

Above: One of the little gardens contained within the house. They were like outdoor rooms, in which you could stroll, or read in the shade of a portico. The gardens were positioned so that you could hear fountains and catch a glimpse of flowers as you went about the house.

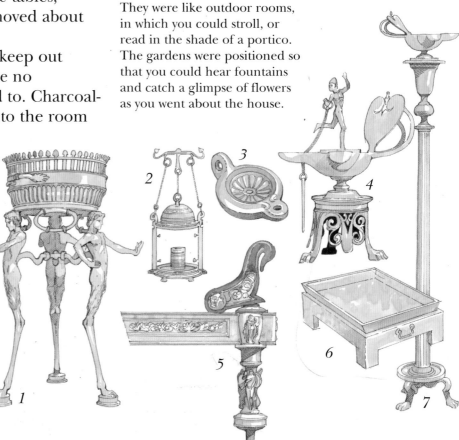

1. A bronze brazier on a stand in the shape of three fauns. 2. A bronze lantern. 3. A terracotta oil lamp used by both rich and poor people. It has a handle at one side and a nozzle for the wick at the other. Olive oil was poured in through the central hole. A wick floated in the oil, with one end coming out through the nozzle to be lit.
4. A lamp with a pin for cleaning out the wick. 5. A corner of a bed, showing part of the leg and headrest. 6. A portable brazier.
7. A bronze lampstand.

Above: Reception rooms. When the Romans relaxed they reclined on couches. They used few chairs, which were reserved for important people. Slaves and children used stools.

Below: Bedrooms. At bottom left, a chamber pot and a strongbox for storing valuables.

15

THE BATHS

ONLY RICH PEOPLE had baths in their homes, but most towns had several sets of public baths. These were lively meeting places where all sorts of people mingled, to exercise and chat as well as bathe.

The baths at the owner's villa could be entered from the house or from the garden. There was a large shady portico outside the door leading in from the garden. This was the ideal place for strenuous exercise before a bath, and very pleasant to relax in afterwards.

The baths themselves had several rooms. A changing room, with a small swimming pool and lavatories, led into the main rooms of the baths – the hot room, the cold room, and the *tepidarium* or warm room, which lessened the shock of passing from hot to cold. The rooms could be used in any order, but it was usual to end with a plunge in the cold bath. Slaves always attended the bathers, to carry towels and toilet things, to oil and massage them and rub them dry.

The farm kitchen and the furnaces were next to the hot bath, but there was no connecting door. The baths were not used by the slaves. When the family was away the furnaces (top right) were not lit.

Right: Bathing equipment.
1. Oil flask decorated with African faces. 2. Pan for cold water for refreshing splashes in the hot bath. 3. Bronze toilet set. 4. Strigils (scrapers) and oil flask on a ring. 5. Tweezers. 6. Nail cleaner. 7. Ear scoop.

Left: The lavatory next to the baths had a marble bench with several holes. Running water flowed under the bench. People cleaned themselves with a sponge on the end of a stick and rinsed it afterwards in a channel of water in front of them.

Left: Stoking the furnace, which heated a large tank of water above it. This tank drew a constant supply of cold water from underground storage cisterns. It took a long time to heat the water. The furnace was kept burning throughout the family's stay. A pipe took the heated water to the hot bath. The water in the bath circulated against the side wall of the furnace, and this kept it warm.

Above: The hot bath chamber, where impurities were sweated out of the skin. A slave is rubbing the owner's wife's skin with olive oil, and then scraping it off her with an instrument called a strigil. This was the way the Romans kept clean. They knew about soap, but did not use it.

THE VILLA RUSTICA

Many Roman writers were interested in farming and several books of farming advice have survived (see page 45). They give detailed instructions on the best way of planning a farm. The kitchen and stables were to be placed where they would catch the winter sun. Everything to do with wine-making needed a cool position, while oil-making needed warmth. Grain storage was a great problem. Despite precautions like siting the granary so that the prevailing wind would keep it dry, grain tended to go mouldy. Fungicides had not yet been invented. Magic methods were tried, such as nailing a toad over the granary door.

In front of the wine pressroom was a walled-off area where newly pressed wine was stored. It was put to mature in jars sunk to their necks in earth to keep cool.

THE FARM BUILDINGS are grouped around a large yard away from the main house, with its own gate. The overseer and his wife live in rooms next to the gate so that they can always see who comes in and goes out. They keep a sharp eye open to make sure nobody is leaving the farm without permission, or pilfering anything to sell in the town. The tool store is close to the overseer's quarters, for the same reason. Pigs and poultry are kept in the yard to protect them from outside raiders. Just in front of the big storage barn is the threshing floor, an area of beaten earth where the animals are made to tread the grain. An open shelter along the side of the barn provides a temporary dry place for the grain if there is a sudden burst of rain during threshing.

Most of the slaves live in a row of rooms on the far side of the court. Some sleep where they work, because it is convenient. The cook sleeps in the big farm kitchen and the baker in the bakehouse. The flour mill and bakery are near the kitchen but in a separate building in the yard. Another group of buildings houses the smithy, the pottery, the weaving room and the joiner's workshop.

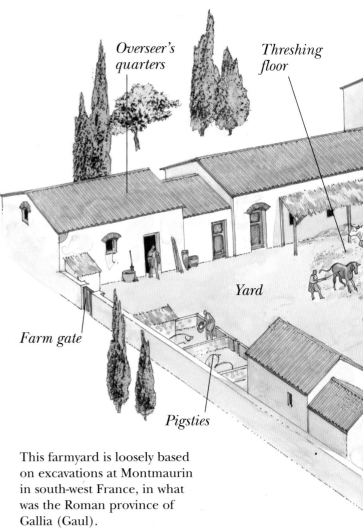

Overseer's quarters

Threshing floor

Yard

Farm gate

Pigsties

This farmyard is loosely based on excavations at Montmaurin in south-west France, in what was the Roman province of Gallia (Gaul).

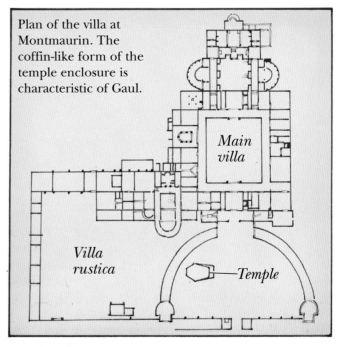

Plan of the villa at Montmaurin. The coffin-like form of the temple enclosure is characteristic of Gaul.

Main villa

Villa rustica

Temple

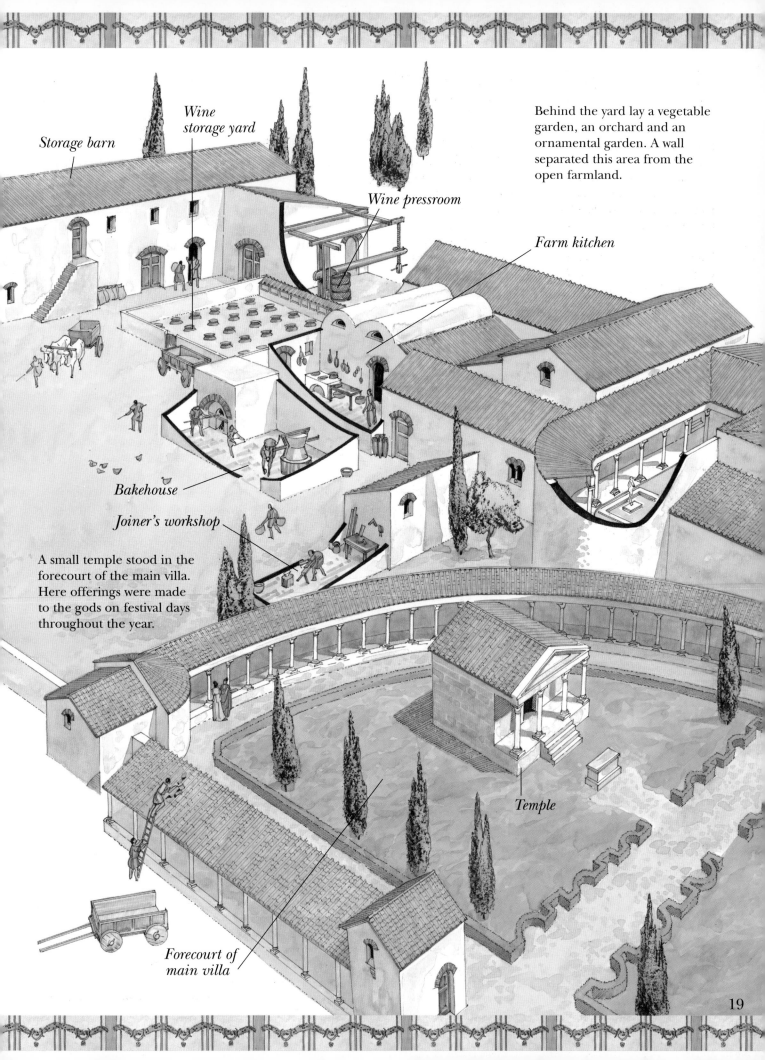

Storage barn

Wine storage yard

Wine pressroom

Behind the yard lay a vegetable garden, an orchard and an ornamental garden. A wall separated this area from the open farmland.

Farm kitchen

Bakehouse

Joiner's workshop

A small temple stood in the forecourt of the main villa. Here offerings were made to the gods on festival days throughout the year.

Temple

Forecourt of main villa

19

A DAY WITH THE FAMILY

LIFE IN THE VILLA starts at daybreak. To the Romans, a day meant the time during which it was light. They saw no point in doing things after dark, for they had only dim oil lamps. People got up at dawn and went to bed at sundown. The day was divided into twelve hours, which meant that in summer, when there was more daylight, the hours were longer than in winter. People took this for granted and were not confused by it. They did not have watches or clocks of the kind we know, but they knew from the position of the sun how much of the day had passed, and timed what they did accordingly.

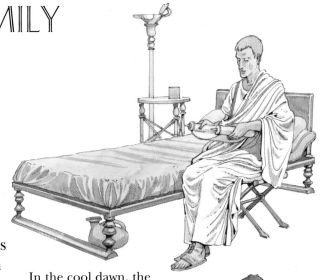

In the cool dawn, the owner likes to slip into a cloak and sandals, and read in his bedroom.

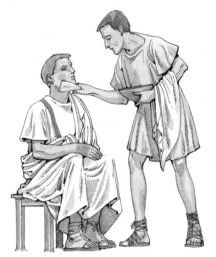

After a breakfast of bread, honey and olives, brought to his room, the owner is shaved.

The daily ceremony at the *lararium*, a shrine in the house at which the family's ancestors were honoured. Incense was burned there daily.

Lessons. Exercises were scratched with a stylus on wax-coated boards, which were smoothed over and used again.

Left: The owner wants to see how work is progressing, so from the third to the fifth hour he tours the villa with the overseer.

A music lesson for the elder daughter.

Below: Afternoon exercise. Today, to keep fit, the owner plays ball with his son.

Above: Midday lunch at the sixth hour. The owner has a light meal brought to him in the library.

The seventh hour, siesta time. In the summer people rested in the hottest part of the day.

The owner's wife spends time on her appearance. Also shown are her armband, hand-mirror and ivory hairpins.

Left: After exercise, a bath. This was the daily routine.

Below: The main meal was eaten from the ninth hour on. Romans lay on sloping couches to eat. The owner is dictating a letter to his secretary.

The owner spends much of the morning on farm business. His wife does not take much interest in this, though many independent Roman women owned and ran their own villas. The younger children spend the morning with their tutor, who is a combination of teacher, guardian and servant. He looks after them now they are too old for a nurse, and takes them to school when they are in Rome. In the afternoon they explore the farm and play with the slave children, while their sister makes friends with the girls in the weaving room. At the end of the day the family dines together.

THE GARDEN

FROM THE POINT OF VIEW of the owner and his family the villa was a place to relax in. The owner did not have to think about city business. Unless he was receiving an official visitor, he would leave off the heavy woollen toga that free citizens always wore in Rome, and put on a simple tunic. If he wished, he could while away the time in the garden, a cool, refreshing place in which the family spent many hours. We know from a letter that a wealthy Roman wrote to a friend in about AD 100, describing his villa garden, that such gardens could be large and elaborately designed. The letter tells of terraces with beds edged with clipped evergreens and tree-lined walks with ivy hanging in garlands from trunk to trunk. As villa owners came mostly in the summer months, the gardens were designed to give coolness and shade. Amidst the flowers and evergreen shrubs fountains sparkled and splashed.

Strolling in the garden. At the end of the walk there is an open-air dining room.

Gardens of the past are much more difficult to recreate than houses, as they do not leave anything solid in the soil for archaeologists to find. There may be some clues. Pollen surviving for centuries in the earth can show what plants were there. At Pompeii researchers have made plaster casts of vanished tree roots, which show as holes in the lava that solidified around them. But all this is a long way from telling us what the gardens really looked like. Roman courtyard gardens have been excavated at Pompeii. They show that the Romans liked to arrange beds and paths in a formal plan, though they did not always do so. Roman wall paintings show paths bordered with lattice fencing, beyond which lie beds of mingled flowers and shrubs. They also show lattice enclosures, with statues and fountains set at regular intervals.

Left: Roman flowers (top to bottom): Iris, crown daisy, oleander and rose.

The rose was the Romans' best-loved flower. They made rose gardens just as we do. Lilies, violets, anemones and poppies were also favourites. Myrtle and oleander were grown for their flowers and evergreen leaves, and box bushes for clipping into fancy shapes. Cypresses and planes were favourite trees. One rich Roman was so fond of his plane trees that he watered them with wine.

THE OVERSEER

A GOOD OVERSEER was vital to the smooth running of a villa. He had to know all about farming, and although he was a slave he had to control the other slaves as if he were their master. An owner expected his overseer to run the farm throughout the year and see that all the jobs were done on time. He had to order supplies and keep accounts. He had to see to the sale of the oil and wine, and keep a record of which purchasers had paid their bills and which still owed money. He had to arrange for surplus fruit and vegetables to be sold and for lambs to be auctioned. No wonder an efficient and honest overseer was one of his master's most valued possessions.

The overseer's wife ran the slave household. She kept the keys to the storerooms; no-one could take food, clothing or blankets without her permission. She directed the baker and the cook and organised the cheese making, food preserving and the weaving of cloth. She also had to see that the main villa was in order.

A clever overseer often knew better than his owner how big a profit the estate could make. However, he would have been foolish to tell. The owner might be satisfied with a lower amount, which would mean that the overseer did not have to work so hard.

The overseer and his wife standing in the doorway of their home.

Their rooms open onto the courtyard next to the big farm gate.

Above: The overseer's accounts are inspected by the owner. If profit is low he will ask why. Perhaps slaves have been sick or the weather bad, or oil may have fallen in price.

Left: At dawn, the overseer gives the foremen their orders and calls for the stable-hands to bring out the oxen and carts. He unlocks the farm gate and leads the gangs into the fields. He will be the last person in at dusk, to lock the gate again.

The overseer's wife weighs out raw wool to be spun during the day.

At night she will check that the weight of the spun yarn is the same.

Stores and equipment are constantly checked to prevent pilfering.

Grain is measured by pouring it into a container of standard size.

Below: Hiring a gang of workers to help out at a busy time. The overseer must be sure they are honest. He will be blamed if they steal anything.

Pickling and preserving fruit for the winter is the responsibility of the overseer's wife.

She also hands out new clothes. Old ones are cut up to make patchwork garments.

THE FARMING YEAR

IN CENTRAL ITALY the soil is thin and the summers hot, with little rain. Roman farmers had a struggle to keep the land moist and fertile. Land that had grown a crop had to be allowed to rest the next year or two, to regain fertility. This land was ploughed several times a year to bury the weeds, which rotted and fed the soil. All this slowed evaporation. The owner's farm grew just enough wheat to provide flour for the villa bakery. Wheat was not very profitable because it could be imported cheaply from other parts of the empire. The best profit came from the vineyard and olive groves. Vegetables and hay were also grown. Moister land by the stream provided grass for spring grazing.

January Vine props and ties are checked. Fruit trees are grafted. The lean oxen have nothing left to eat but acorns, ivy or salted straw.

February The vines begin to show green shoots and must be pruned. Vegetables grown between the vine rows are weeded.

March Ploughing the fallow (resting) land for the first time. The plough has a metal ploughshare that makes furrows easily in the light soil.

April The sheep are sheared. Shearing is done in the hottest part of the day, when the sun makes the oily fleeces soft and easy to handle.

May An ox, a sheep and a pig are led around the estate and sacrificed to the god Mars amid prayers for the wellbeing of the farm.

June The hay is cut, to be stored and fed to the cattle later in the year. Their pastures are dried up, but they can eat leaves for a while.

By midsummer the animals' grazing land was shrivelled up. Few cows were kept. Milk came from sheep and goats. During the summer shepherds had to take the sheep away to cooler pastures in the mountains to find grass. This deprived the farm grassland of precious manure from the sheep droppings, which added to the farmers' problems.

The Romans knew that land becomes exhausted if nothing is returned to the soil. Compost was made from manure and vegetable waste, and from the mush left over from olive pressing. The outflow from the lavatory drains was also used. The Romans also valued 'green manuring' – ploughing a crop into the soil to rot and enrich it.

July Harvest time. The reapers cut the corn and bind it into sheaves to be taken to the farm. The stubble is burned to enrich the soil.

August Threshing. The corn is spread out over the threshing floor and animals are driven around on it, to trample the grain out of the ears.

September Treading the newly picked grapes. The first juices flow out into jars. The pulp that remains in the vat will go to the wine press.

October Lambing. Sheep are mated early in the year, so that the lambs, born in the autumn, will not have to bear the hot sun.

November Next year's wheat and barley crops are sown in the spaces between the olive trees. The ploughman covers the seed.

December Olive picking. Care is taken not to bruise them. Boughs out of reach are struck with canes so that the fruit falls onto cloths.

SLAVES AT WORK

A SMALL VILLA might have only a few slaves. A large one might have thirty to forty, or even more. On villas of similar size the number of slaves varied according to the type of farming done. The owner of the villa described in this book needed quite a lot of slaves because he grew a wide variety of crops, made wine and oil, and kept some sheep as well. Other landowners chose to specialise. Some had huge estates on which they only reared sheep. They needed fewer slaves. But whether they had lots of farm slaves or just a few, owners wanted to be sure they were getting good value from them.

Slave quarters have survived at only a few villas. They were small rooms that may have had many beds.

Bread goes into the oven to be baked, while the donkey harnessed to the corn mill trudges around and around to turn it.

Above: The smithy on a winter day. The overseer knows that field hands like to linger here and warm up when it is cold outside.

Left: In the mountains the shepherds make huts to live in. They have to protect the flocks from wolves and robbers.

Right: The potter's jars do all the jobs that plastic, tins and glass bottles do for us.

Above: The joiner is kept busy making and repairing carts, sheds, gates and window shutters.

Above: The farm kitchen. The slaves' food is rationed. Those who do heavy work get more.

Below: Clearing out drainage ditches so that sudden heavy cloudbursts will not wash away the soil.

Below: Carrying manure from the compost heap to be put around the vines in winter.

Above: A farm hand takes the pigs to the woods to eat acorns. When they need to be fattened they will get beans and corn.

Below: Heaving grain up the granary steps. Farm hands do the work that needs more muscle than skill.

Slaves were expensive. They had to be fed and clothed all year round. They could not be laid off when the weather was bad, as hired workers were. Like expensive machinery in a modern factory, they had to be used all the time in order to justify the amount spent on them. Villas kept their own craftsmen so that the right person would be on hand when things needed mending, and work need never stop. In winter time when days were short, farm slaves, unlike everyone else, had to work before dawn and after dark, on such jobs as sharpening stakes and making baskets, hampers and beehives.

VINES AND OLIVES

THE GRAPE HARVEST is the busiest time of the year. Extra people have to be hired so that the grapes can be gathered quickly, while they are at their best. The villa produces very good wine. The soil and site are just right – a sheltered hillside, not too hot or dry, which gets heavy dews and no rough winds. Though vines need a lot of attention they are well worth it for the price the wine fetches. They have to be very skilfully pruned. Left to themselves vines becomes huge rambling plants with lots of leaves and only a few grapes. Roman vine dressers pruned the top roots of the vines, and three times a year they broke up the soil around the plants to let air and moisture reach the roots.

Olives were also a valuable crop. The Romans used olive oil as a source of light in their lamps, as a food in the place of butter since milk was not plentiful, and as a body lotion at the baths. The owner of the villa means to plant more olives, but he will have to wait a long time before he gets a crop. Olive trees grow very slowly. To avoid having no income for many years from the land planted with olives, Roman farmers grew wheat or barley between the trees.

The pickers gather the grapes in small baskets, which they empty into a big basketwork container, mounted on wheels to be pulled to the treading vat. The overseer is watching to see that the job is done properly. The grape pickers are supposed to lift the bunches with iron hooks and cut them off with grape-cutting knives or small sickles. These have to be ready, well sharpened, or else the pickers may start pulling off the bunches by hand, which scatters the fruit on the ground.

Vines were propped up on wooden stakes and cross-pieces of reeds tied together with willow shoots, or on specially trained trees, often black poplar or elm.

Fruit growers' tools:
1. Fruit baskets.
2. Wooden bucket.
3. Pruning knives.
4. Grape knife.
5. Grape cutters.
6. Pronged drag-hoes.
7. Mattocks for breaking soil.
8. Weeding hoe.
9. Spades.

Picking green olives, which were gathered in the autumn, before the main crop. They were good for eating; the black olives made the best oil. Olives were pickled in brine to be stored and used throughout the year.

GRAPE JUICE turns into wine if yeasts from the skins are allowed to change its natural sugar into alcohol. The first step is to squeeze the juice out of the grapes. The Romans began this by treading on them. This brought out the first juices but there was still a lot left in the remaining pulp. This juice was forced out in a wine press. The juice was then stored in large jars to let the yeast work and the wine mature.

Below: In the wine storage yard, a buyer is sampling wine from one of the big sunken jars in which it has been maturing.

His assistants are carrying off some wine he has already bought.

Grape treaders from a carving. They were told to keep their clothes

tightly belted to stop sweat trickling down their backs into the juice.

Oxskin

Press-beam

Rush containers

Screw

Vat

Above: The pressroom, cut away to show the press. The pulp, in rush containers, is under the long press-beam, which slaves are winding down. The juice is channelled into a long vat in the yard. Then it is piped to the jars through holes in the side of the vat.

Wine was ladled from the storage jars into long, narrow wine jars (you can see one being carried in the picture opposite), to finish maturing in the wine loft, or to be sold. Wine was also sold in bulk, direct from the vat, and delivered in an oxskin (there is one on wheels in the yard, opposite). Customers could even buy grapes while they were still on the vine, have the wine made at the villa, and collect it afterwards.

Oil making was a complicated process. The olive stones had to be separated from the olives before they could be pressed. They first went into a crushing mill, which gently squashed them without cracking the stones, and produced a stoneless pulp. When this was pressed it gave out a liquid that had to be poured from one pan to another as many as thirty times, to separate the pure oil from the lees (dregs).

The olive pressing room. A cartload of newly picked olives is being brought in. These will have to be cleaned, and steeped in hot water to soften them. Then they will be ready for the crushing mill. This is a deep stone basin in which two crushing stones are set so that they revolve without touching the sides. The stones are turned by slaves. The juice from the oil-press (which can be seen in the background) flows into jars sunk in the pressroom floor. The oil in the juice starts to rise to the top. A slave is skimming this oil off into another jar. It will then be clarified to make pure oil.

THE LIFE OF A SLAVE

THE SLAVES at the owner's villa were almost all born there, but their ancestors had come from many different lands. Some had been captured in Spain or Greece as prisoners of war. Some had been taken prisoner around the Black Sea or in the eastern Mediterranean, and sold by pirates. As time went on, most slaves were the children of slave parents.

Slaves were completely in the power of their owners, who could inflict any punishment they wished on them, even death. By the time of the empire very harsh punishments were beginning to be thought unreasonable, and slaves were treated better. Household slaves were sometimes almost part of the family. Their children might be brought up with the owner's children and share their education. A clever slave could have a bright future, perhaps becoming his owner's close friend.

Generous owners gave their slaves allowances of money. If they saved this for many years they might be able to buy their freedom. In Imperial times it was quite common to set a slave free after many years' good service. Slaves in the country were less fortunate than those in town. They had few chances to get any money to buy their freedom and they worked long, hard hours.

Many of the villa slaves have stories to tell of how their grandparents were kidnapped in far lands and auctioned in the slave markets.

When slaves grew dearer, ruthless Roman landowners obtained them by waylaying passing travellers.

Working in chains is a punishment for troublesome slaves.

Some villas have prisons for them. Only the owner decides their release.

Hardworking slaves are rewarded by being given their own patch of land to cultivate.

A mother of four children is set free as a reward. She wears a cap of liberty. Owners want women to have children as this produces slaves to sell.

The owner encourages his slaves by listening to suggestions from them.

Right: Sick slaves are well cared for. In the past many owners sold off sick slaves. In Imperial times owners are kinder. They take as much care of a sick slave as of a sick ox.

Below: August 13 was a holiday for all slaves. The day was sacred to the goddess Diana whose temple had been a refuge for runaway slaves. The villa slaves have a day off in the town and enjoy the public baths.

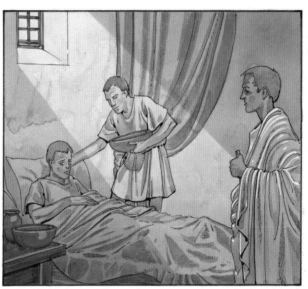

Old slaves are no longer sold off in Imperial times. They do odd jobs and are looked after for the rest of their lives.

GOING TO MARKET

THE NEW VILLA has the advantage of being fairly near a good-sized town, where essential supplies can be bought and farm produce sold. It is quite easy to walk there and back in a day, and still have enough time to do business. This is ideal when there are sheep to take to auction or oxskins of wine to deliver, for it means that the slave in charge does not have to be away overnight, a thing which the owner is always keen to avoid.

The overseer has sent one of his most reliable foremen to town with a donkey-load of asparagus from the kitchen garden. He has to see which greengrocer will give him the best price for it. The foreman has brought his young daughter along. While he does the villa business she will try to sell a couple of hens and some cabbages that they have brought along on their own account. These have come from the small piece of land the foreman is allowed to cultivate.

Below: The *forum*, or main town square. All the town's important public buildings are grouped around it. These include the main temple, the offices of the town government and a large building called a *basilica*, which houses the law courts and is also the place where businessmen meet to arrange deals. There are shops and offices all around. The town is surrounded by a wall in which there are several gates.

Before they go back to the villa, the foreman and his daughter may be tempted to spend a little of their hard-earned money at the cooked-food shop near the forum. Spicy meat pasties are a change from farm rations.

Below: The entrance to the temple. Inside, two rows of columns hold up the roof.

The forum is the place to come to learn the local news and political gossip. It is usually full of shoppers and businessmen hurrying about. On market days traders set up their stalls there and it is crowded and noisy.

The town is quite large. It has its own theatre, which, like most Greek and Roman theatres, is in the open air. It also has an amphitheatre for gladiator fights, and there are several sets of public baths. As most people take a daily bath, the public baths are like social clubs where people meet friends.

The narrow streets of the town are lined with houses, shops and craftsmen's workplaces. There are also many taverns and small bars.

A RAINY DAY

IN CENTRAL ITALY rain can come suddenly, in torrents. Today it looks as though it may rain all day. The overseer's wife said yesterday that rain was on its way. She had seen the ducks fly up from the pond in a rush and perch on the roof of the barn. That's a sure sign of wet weather.

Inside the main villa it is warm and comfortable. The owner's wife has told the overseer to arrange for the small furnace that heats the winter dining room to be lit, and she has asked for braziers to be brought into the other rooms, to take off the autumn chill. She likes to warm her toes by a fire.

Outside, the slaves work in the pouring rain. There are lots of jobs that can be done no matter what the weather is like, if the men are well wrapped up. Some work can only be done in the wet. Gangs are sent around the estate to see if there are any leaks in the tiled drainage channels which collect the rainwater and take it where it is needed. The leaky places have a cross marked on them with a piece of charcoal so that the cracked tiles can be replaced later.

This evening the outdoor workers may get extra rations to keep away chills. It would be false economy to let the slaves become ill.

Jobs for a rainy day, from a Roman farming book: cleaning and pitching (waterproofing) storage jars; cleaning out farm buildings; shifting grain; hauling out manure; starting a new compost heap; mending harnesses and making new ones; cleaning seed (grain or other seed that was to be stored for any length of time was sieved to rid it of dirt and pests).

A gang of workers is taking out a load of manure from the compost heap to spread it over land that is waiting to be planted this autumn. Others are clearing out a muddy ditch that is blocked and starting to overflow.

They have been issued with wet-weather clothes – long-sleeved leather tunics with hoods, and leather gloves and leggings. Despite this protection, they do not keep as dry as the overseer, who directs them from a portico.

Inside the house the sound of rain pattering into the pool in the atrium is a cheerful reminder of how nice it is to be inside. The children are racing their hoops around the pool.

Their mother and elder sister are lying on couches, eating figs and honey cakes. The owner is in the library planning a book he means to write about the pleasures of life in the country.

FRIENDS TO STAY

FRIENDS FROM ROME have come to stay at the villa and a dinner party is being given in their honour. Like many rich Romans the owner and his wife are extremely fond of good food. They have been planning the menu with the chef. We might think that they have ordered enough food for a banquet, but by wealthy Roman standards the meal is quite modest. For the first course there are various salads served with mint and olives, together with a dish of snails and fish garnished with sliced eggs and rue. Next the guests can choose from a variety of meat dishes – roast kid, pheasant, goose, ham and sows' udders. After that, guests will be offered a dessert of fruit and nuts.

There are nine diners, three to each couch. A larger number would be rather squashed. The dishes are brought in a few at a time and set on the table. During the meal dinner guests are often entertained with readings, music or jokes, according to their tastes. Tonight a juggler is amusing the guests. After the meal the guests, with garlands of flowers on their heads, will continue talking and drinking the villa's excellent wine.

Above: The kitchen. The cooking is done over wood or charcoal fires, which are kindled in the worktop of the brick oven. Fuel is stored in the big arch underneath. Food was simmered, or grilled on gridirons.

Kitchen equipment:
1. Bronze ladle.
2. Bronze strainer.
3. Mould for cooking six pies or buns.
4. Wooden spoon.
5. Bronze pan.
6. Earthenware pot with lid.
7. Bronze basin.
8. Spoon.
9. Knives
10. Gridiron (to be set over the fire).

To cook a flamingo (a Roman recipe): Pluck the flamingo, wash and truss it and put it in a pan of water. Season with dill and a little vinegar and put to simmer. When half cooked, add leeks and coriander. Thicken the cooking liquid to make a sauce and flavour this with crushed pepper, caraway, coriander, asafoetida root, mint and rue. Add Jericho dates, pour over the bird and serve. The same recipe can also be used for cooking parrot.

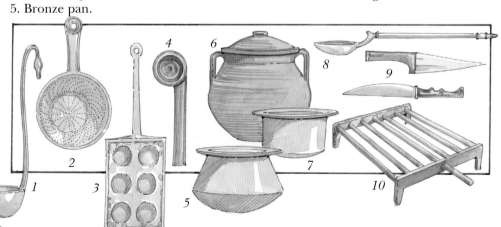

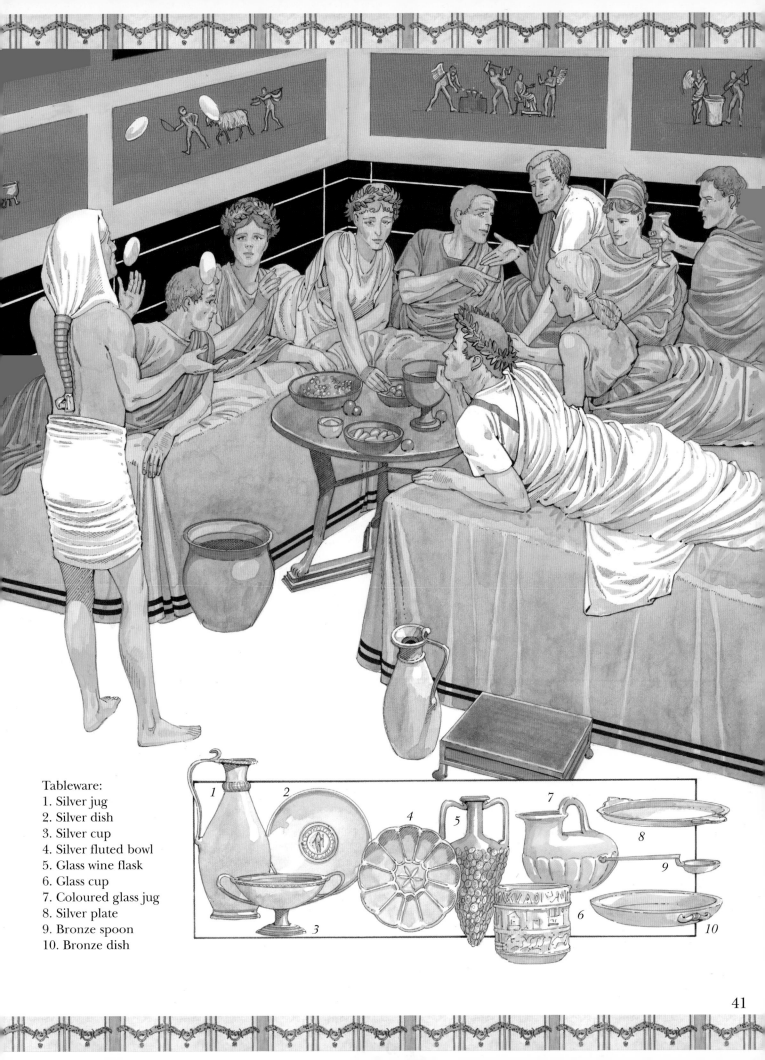

Tableware:
1. Silver jug
2. Silver dish
3. Silver cup
4. Silver fluted bowl
5. Glass wine flask
6. Glass cup
7. Coloured glass jug
8. Silver plate
9. Bronze spoon
10. Bronze dish

FESTIVITIES

THROUGHOUT THE YEAR Roman country people held festivals that were connected with the seasons and the growth of the crops. Some of these were celebrations to thank the gods for work that had been successfully completed – the autumn ploughing finished or the grapes harvested – and some were ceremonies to gain the gods' favour and ask for protection against drought, diseases and evil spirits.

It was usual to make an offering of food and drink to the god whose festival it was. At the time of the grape harvest Bacchus, the wine god, was honoured. When the corn was all cut, thanks were given to Ceres, goddess of grain. February 23 was the festival of Terminus, the god of the boundaries. Farmers were very apt to quarrel over where their boundaries lay, and on this day anger was forgotten and neighbours' quarrels made up.

The festival of Terminus. The god was represented by a boundary post which was set up as a landmark where two estates met. It often had two heads, one looking each way. The owner and his family have come to meet their neighbours and honour the god together. They have made an altar, and the owner tosses corn three times into the fire. The children have brought pieces of honeycomb to offer.

Portable brazier

The biggest festival of the year was the Saturnalia, in December. All the rules were turned upside down. Slaves had a holiday and were waited on by their masters. The festival probably grew out of the country custom of celebrating the end of the autumn ploughing. By Imperial times it had grown into an annual merry-making in town and country alike. There was much feasting and people exchanged presents.

Saturnalia at the villa. This year the owner and his family have decided to spend the holiday at the villa and celebrate it in the old-fashioned country way. At the start of the festival dice are thrown to see who is to be this year's Saturnalia king. The king rules throughout the holiday, and everyone has to obey his commands, even if he asks them to do something very ridiculous indeed.

The slaves and their king are enjoying a feast. For once in the year they can have as much wine and food as they wish. The owner and his family are helping to hand around the dishes. They are having to be servants today. The slaves are pleased to see them there. They think their new owners are kind and just, and by Roman standards they are. Today everyone at the villa is happy together.

TIMESPAN

753 BC Legendary date of Rome's founding.

509 BC Rome becomes a republic.

264–146 BC Three wars with Carthage are fought, establishing Rome's power abroad.

c.150 BC Cato writes *De Agricultura*, the earliest discussion of Roman farming.

73 BC Slave rebellion led by Spartacus, a gladiator.

37 BC Varro publishes *De Re Rustica*, on all aspects of farming. The first volume deals with field crops, the second with animal rearing, and the third with the raising of fish, birds and snails for the luxury market, and also with bee-keeping. The first volume was written for Varro's wife Fundania, who had recently bought her own estate.

27 BC Augustus becomes first Roman emperor.

c.AD 50 Columella writes twelve volumes on farming, to show owners of large estates how to control costs. He had already written a book on crops and trees, part of which is lost. A few years later Pliny the Elder (so called because his nephew Pliny was also a writer) finishes an encyclopedia of the natural world. He includes discussions of farming.

AD 79 The volcano Vesuvius erupts, burying the towns of Herculaneum and Pompeii. Their excavated remains tell us a great deal about Roman houses, furniture and gardens.

ROMAN FACTS

Fourteen was the average age of a Roman girl at her first marriage, so our villa owner's daughter may have been about to marry. Rich parents decided whom their children should marry, though by Imperial times they did not insist on choosing, if they were kind.

Slaves sometimes joined forces against their owners. There were organised rebellions, but the slaves were defeated by the better organisation of the free Romans.

The Romans were well aware of the threat their slaves posed. When someone suggested that slaves ought to wear different clothes from free citizens, the reply was, 'No, for then they will see how many there are of them and how few of us.' Even in kinder Imperial times, the law stated that if a slave killed his owner, every slave in the household was to be put to death on the grounds that they should have prevented the crime.

An exceedingly wealthy Roman built a villa at Tivoli, just outside Rome, that had gilded ceilings and running water in every bedroom. A villa that was close to a town and was not really a farm was known as a *villa suburbana*.

Frequent laws were passed to curb extravagant spending on food. In 115 BC dormice, shellfish and imported birds were forbidden, but all these laws were ignored.

Pliny the Younger, who wrote about his garden in the letter mentioned on page 22, had box bushes clipped into the shapes of the letters of his name.

Notes from farming authors

A tall story: A Roman pig breeder boasted of rearing a sow so fat that a shrew ate a hole in its flesh and brought up a family in it.

Lucky and unlucky days: The 6th day of the month is very unfavourable for plants. The 11th and 12th are good for sheep-shearing and harvesting. The 13th should be avoided for sowing but is good for transplanting seedlings. The 30th is the best day for looking over work and dealing out supplies. The 1st, 4th and 7th are sacred days.

Rules for grape-treaders: Wash your feet. Do not eat or drink while treading. Do not climb in and out of the grape vat more than is necessary.

How to manage slaves: Put them to work in gangs of not more than ten, so that they are easy to control. When buying slaves avoid those that are too timid or too boisterous. Do not have too many slaves of the same nationality, as this leads to squabbles.

A way to store grapes: Put them in a vessel with boiled water. Treat the vessel with pitch and seal with gypsum. Store in a cool place. The water can be given to the sick.

Storing other fruit: Figs, apples, plums and pears should be stored in honey, with their stalks removed, and not touching.

Oak trees and olives: A farmer claimed his neighbour's oak trees were making his olive grove barren. The oak and the olive are enemies.

Some tips: A piece of oak wood in the centre of the manure heap will prevent harmful snakes from hiding in it. Grape skins left over from the wine press can be soaked in water to make a drink for the slaves. The watery lees from the olive press make a good weedkiller.

Give the unhealthy work to hired gangs. Do not risk the slaves getting ill.

Check that your overseer has not been letting out the oxen for hire, or charging for more seed than he has sown, or stealing your grain.

A shepherd should drive his sheep westwards until midday, and then eastwards, so that they do not have the sun in their eyes. He should stop the pregnant ewes from lagging behind and the young ones from skipping ahead, but not by throwing things at them. He should shout and use his crook instead.

Weather signs: Rain – cattle look up; centipedes swarm up the walls; hens peck their lice off energetically. Storm – fleas bite more vigorously; moths gather in the flame of the lamp; there are sparks in the fire around the cauldron. Fine weather – the night owl sings; lamps burn clearly; cranes fly a straight course.

Rules for olive pickers: Do not use gloves; this bruises the fruit. To get the top olives, beat the branches, not the fruit. Use a reed, not a stiff pole. Do not shake the fruit down – pick it.

Glossary

Amphitheatre An oval building with a central arena and tiers of seats, designed for the staging of gladiator contests.

Asafoetida A Middle Eastern herb used in medicine and cookery.

Atrium (plural **atria**) The main room of a Roman house in early times. It was characterised by an inward-sloping roof with a square central opening, and a corresponding pool in the floor to collect rainwater. By Imperial times a house might have an atrium and other reception rooms as well. The villa at Montmaurin had two atria.

Basilica A rectangular building with a large central area and two side aisles, each divided from it by a row of columns. Basilicas were built as public meeting places for merchants and business people. When Christianity became the official religion of the Roman empire in the 4th century AD, churches were built in basilica form.

Bond To cause particles of matter to cling together in a mass.

Box shrub A small-leaved evergreen shrub, used for hedging, and often clipped into fancy shapes.

Brazier A portable container in which a fire is burned. The Romans burned charcoal in their braziers.

Brine Salt water.

Cement A paste of water, sand and lime, which sets on drying. The Romans used it in building.

Charcoal Partly burned wood, used as a fuel.

Cistern A large container for water.

Clarify To make a liquid clear by removing impurities.

Colonnade A series of columns at regular intervals, forming a linked row.

Crane A stork-like bird.

Dividers A pair of compasses for drawing circles or comparing short measurements of length.

Faun An imaginary creature in the form of a man with small horns and the tail of a goat. The Romans thought of these creatures as spirits inhabiting the countryside.

Forum A large open area in the centre of a Roman town, where important public meetings were held. It was also a marketplace.

Gladiator A person, usually a slave, trained to take part in armed contests (using deadly weapons) for the amusement of an audience of spectators. Fights were often to the death.

Graft To insert a small shoot from a plant (that is to be cultivated) into a slit in the stem of a stronger, coarser variety of the same plant. The shoots of the host plant are cut back, leaving the inserted shoot to flourish on the strength of the other's roots.

Granary A building in which grain is stored.

Imperial times The period when Romans were ruled by emperors, from 27 BC to the fall of the western Roman empire in AD 476.

Joiner A woodworker who makes furniture and fittings.

Lararium A small shrine containing statuettes representing the guardian spirits of the

household. These were the souls of family ancestors whose influence was thought to safeguard the health and prosperity of the family. All big Roman houses had a lararium, usually in the atrium, and daily ceremonies were performed in front of it.

Lees The dregs of a liquid, containing unwanted refuse.

Limestone A light-coloured, easily cut rock, much used for building.

Mosaic A decorative surface for floors and walls, made by setting tiny cubes of coloured stone or glass into a base of freshly applied mortar while it is still soft.

Nymphaeum An ornamental courtyard in which water, in the form of pools or fountains, plays an important part. It was dedicated to the nymphs, or water spirits.

Papyrus Paper made from the papyrus reed.

Pitch A resinous substance, runny when heated, which was used to seal the inside of porous pottery containers.

Ploughshare The pointed metal blade of a plough that cuts a furrow in the earth.

Plumbline A length of thread, weighted at the end with a piece of lead. When it is allowed to hang freely it provides a true vertical line.

Portico A porch or covered walk, with a roof supported by a row of columns.

Preserving Treating perishable food so that it will keep in storage.

Press-beam Part of a press for making oil or wine: a long, heavy wooden beam, one end of which was pulled down mechanically, so that the other end exerted pressure on whatever was in the press. The longer the beam, the greater the pressure that could be achieved.

Republican times From the founding of the Roman republic in 509 BC to the beginning of the reign of Augustus in 27 BC.

Rubble Small, irregular pieces of stone.

Sesterce A unit of Roman money.

Smithy A blacksmith's workshop.

Strigil An instrument with a hollow, curved blade, for scraping and cleaning the skin after a hot bath. The skin was oiled, and the oil and perspiration flowed into the hollow.

Tepidarium The room in a set of baths which was kept at a moderate temperature, for massage and resting. The hot room was called the *caldarium*, and the cold room the *frigidarium.*

Terracotta Baked brownish-red clay.

Threshing The process of separating grain from the ears of corn. It was done by trampling the cut corn, or beating it with sticks.

Threshing floor The outdoor area where corn was threshed.

Try-square A wooden or metal guide used by carpenters to check right angles.

Wick A length of twisted fibres almost completely submerged in oil, which it soaks up so that it can be lit at the uncovered end.

Yeasts Microscopic fungi.

INDEX

Page numbers in bold type refer to illustrations.

First published in MCMXCII as *Inside Story – A Roman Villa* by Macdonald Young Books © The Salariya Book Co Ltd MCMXCII

Look out for these other exciting titles from Book House

World of Wonder

David Stewart
HB ISBN: 978-1-905638-24-6
PB ISBN: 978-1-905638-25-3

Danielle Stevens
HB ISBN: 978-1-907184-04-8
PB ISBN: 978-1-907184-05-5

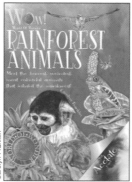

Carolyn Franklin
HB ISBN: 978-1-905638-26-0
PB ISBN: 978-1-905638-27-7

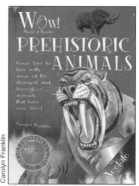

Carolyn Franklin
HB ISBN: 978-1-907184-12-3
PB ISBN: 978-1-907184-13-0

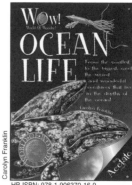

Carolyn Franklin
HB ISBN: 978-1-906370-16-9
PB ISBN: 978-1-906370-17-6

Top 10 Worst

Fiona Macdonald
HB ISBN: 978-1-906714-86-4
PB ISBN: 978-1-906714-87-1

Carolyn Franklin
HB ISBN: 978-1-907184-46-8
PB ISBN: 978-1-907184-47-5

Fiona Macdonald
HB ISBN: 978-1-907184-40-6
PB ISBN: 978-1-907184-41-3

Fiona Macdonald
HB ISBN: 978-1-906714-84-0
PB ISBN: 978-1-906714-85-7

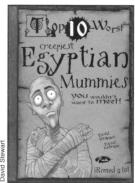

David Stewart
HB ISBN: 978-1-907184-44-4
PB ISBN: 978-1-907184-45-1

Graffex

Bram Stoker/Penko Gelev
PB ISBN: 978-1-905638-52-9

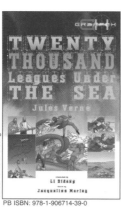

Jules Verne/Li Sidong
PB ISBN: 978-1-906714-39-0

Anon/Li Sidong
PB ISBN: 978-1-906714-73-4

William Shakespeare/Penko Gelev
PB ISBN: 978-1-906714-40-6

Mary Shelley/Penko Gelev
PB ISBN: 978-1-905638-72-7

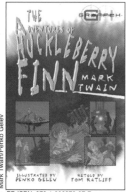

Mark Twain/Penko Gelev
PB ISBN: 978-1-906370-07-7

Jonathan Swift/Penko Gelev
PB ISBN: 978-1-906714-38-3

William Shakespeare/Penko Gelev
PB ISBN: 978-1-906714-72-7

Homer/Li Sidong
PB ISBN: 978-1-906714-37-6

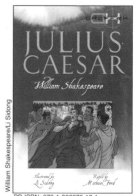

William Shakespeare/Li Sidong
PB ISBN: 978-1-906370-12-1